# With a Little More Feeling

## A poetry collection

Kerry R. Jeffrey

Cover photo courtesy of
Denise Skeldon

Dedicated To:

Brandy Reeder Thompson

To the most wonderful,

beautiful soul that I call my

twin in friendship.

# ....The one that started it all

**Living now**

Pure power
The war ends

The beat hardens
The sounds deaden

To turn upside down
You become upright

To survive
You take no chances

Meet the immortal
Stay the same

The message is gone
Dreams are still here

Now, you are truly living

….Hoping for a moment

**If**

If a friend was a lover,
It would be a thought.
To have someone there,
More often than not.

If your smile cured hearts,
It would heal more than a few.
To have a wonderful skill,
They'd think kindly of you.

If laughter was sweet song,
It would soothe the soul.
You'd have to sing out loud,
Letting my feelings take a stroll.

**Kiss**

I know what would happen,
Just too simply kiss you.
The heart would beat harder;
Emotions will come unglued.

My eyes would press tighter;
Imagination would run wild.
My mind would wander,
With lots of feelings compiled.

My senses would fail;
Blow away with the breeze.
Because I'd want to kiss more,
As often as I please.

**Melt**

I can see beneath my eyes,
You, a sight to behold.
For, I don't want to awaken.
To stay dreaming; with visions
foretold.

I feel safe with your voice,
Like endless, comfort sleep.
Unbridled by sweet words;
Kept forever; treasured deep.

With you, I care immensely;
With compassion, heartfelt.
Making my heart stronger; unbroken.
Making me dream longer; my heart
melts.

**And Then I Think…..**

This heart just skipped; beating harder.
My knees collapsing; admitting defeat.
Just seeing you simply beautiful,
Spins me around, up off my feet.

You're a sight for sore eyes.
Yes, you're an amazing sight.
And I can't help but stare;
I feel as though high as a kite.

You appear in sweet dreams;
Linger within my mind.
You're such a beautiful creature.
Surely, the prettiest of your kind.

**I'm Comfy Here**

I seem to have something of yours.
It seems I have slowly stolen your heart.
Where do I need to begin?
How about the beginning, the very start?

I slipped in through your darkness,
Just to find the happier of places.
Through the back glow of your visions;
Resting in the warmest of spaces.

Held in by your breath;
Captured by a sigh,
For inside your heart I'll stay,
Quiet; silently on standby.

….Love is

**Idea of Love**

If love was an object of sight,
Just what would it be?
Maybe an order to grow,
Just a single tree?

If love was a subject of habit,
Like smoking in a rare form,
Would it be addicting?
Would we want just a little more?

**Love Sick**

Admiration could be a sickness;
It, very well, may be true.
Maybe it's one reason I get weak,
When I smile upon thinking of you.

This possibly explains things;
Why my mind feels most high.
When I hear your name,
I get dizzy; don't know why.

There likely isn't a cure,
But I'm sure I'll be fine.
Maybe just the thought of you,
Leaves me happy; on cloud nine.

**Insight**

I get lost in the color;
Enriched in the hue.
The brightest light tempted,
Trying to outshine you.

They glisten so dramatic;
Dancing with gleam.
They're caressed in a love;
More blue than they seem.

They show the shadows,
Of loves lost before.
Without a doubt,
Have left you scorn.

Your eyes show so much.
An intoxicating gaze.
I can stare forever;
Getting lost from nights into days.

**….On Every Word**

So cute in your words,
Greater said by the lip.
Upon gentle laughter,
Does my imagination slip.

It's beauty behind a smile;
Only tempted by a grin.
Beauty exudes from inside;
Yours could be a sin.

It's tender, soft words said,
That leaves me grinning; delighted.
For just to see you smile,
Would make my heart excited.

**You and I**

I see you through my eyes of hunting,
For like the lion, I search for something.
I wait in great desperation,
For the world is causing my frustration.

I see you through my eyes of caring,
For like the cub, I strive for more.
I see the world different, with little vision,
For the sun will rise and the rain will pour.

You see me through eyes of glitter,
For like the lioness you see things precious.
You wait with all your wonder,
For you are the rain, yet the thunder.

**Wanting to Talk**

If a dew drop fell,
From the tree of you,
Would it change the person,
Or change a few?

Your worries are secrets;
You keep them hidden.
Can you act on them;
Is it forbidden?

I know its complex,
With these things confined.
I want you in happiness,
And with me you'll find.

I'll be here for you,
To listen with heart.
I love you deeply,
Till death do us part.

….You can't be serious

**We Are Young**

Dirty minds and goofy thoughts.
It's what we choose when sanity's lost.

We're all a little crazy and just a little nuts.
At least our ages don't kick our butts.

We have each other and we are simple folk.
At least we can take a silly joke.

## Twenty One

Go have some fun and party down.
Turn a smile and rid a frown.
Go see someone naked and drink
something stout.
Here's hoping they don't have a
snout.
Get a little buzzed but don't overtake.
You never know who'll be there
when you wake.

**Ragu**

I came home but you weren't here.
I called your name but it's nothing I hear.

I'm all alone; all by myself.
There no food upon the shelf.

The more I think, the more I wish,
That I need to prepare a nice hot dish.

"Hey! A sandwich…a pie…some beef stew!"
On second thought maybe pasta to chew.

Just a second, a minute or two,
It's me, my pasta, and a sauce named Ragu.

**Turtles**

Ever watch a turtle?
So lonely; so slow.
Doesn't really do much,
Doesn't put on a show.

He has that tough shell.
He hardly walks.
Does he speak a word?
Does he ever talk?

I guess he doesn't do much,
Just his daily habits.
Except when he races,
And beats stupid rabbits.

**Morning Drag**

So, I'm having a bad morning;
It's already a bad day.
I have surely burnt some toast;
Hey, what can I say?

I think I slept well.
I might have had a dream.
There's a dog under foot!
"Let him out!" I scream.

It's not going too well.
Today is just not my day.
"How are my armpits sticky?"
I just sprayed them with hairspray!

**Kiss Logic**

A kiss on the cheek,
Though soft and warm,
For you feel much better;
Causes no harm.

To give pecks upon necks,
Will make one grin.
Though one on the ear,
Tis sweeter than sin.

Pressing slightly two lips,
For I believe most subtle,
Leaves you tingling for more;
Could get you in trouble.

## Belief

I don't believe in many things;
Some say it's a shame.
To believe in so much,
Really is a pain.

I can't believe in aliens,
They're a little strange.
Because you mess with them;
Your mind, they'll rearrange.

I can't believe in ghosts,
For them I cannot see.
If I met one of them,
My pants, I'd surely pee.

I can't believe in monsters,
For they are much too mean.
Argue with a dragon;
He'll really burn your spleen.

Of all the things I don't believe,
I can say without dispute,
I believe in one thing;
That thing is you.

# ....A pressing matter

**Me**

My life now and forever will be just
a blanketed expression of love for
whom I was meant to be. Something
great!

My soul now and forever will be just
a confused and moral idea that I have
led myself to believe. Something
has to be there.

My body now and forever will be a
statue of a divine figure that's truly
happy but doesn't know how to show
it. Some things remain the same.

**Stereo Typical**

300 eyes staring upon my shadow;
Staring in disarray.
My thoughts are empty,
So why does the corrupt stay?

Thoughts of hurt are acid;
They wrought my moral chains.
I try to think happy,
But the emotions want to complain.

Breathe in for I am air;
Wonderful as a star.
Why don't people see me,
As common as they are?

**Eyes of the Beholder**

In the eyes of the beholder,
In which has become of me,
A mere man can look upon,
Things he'll never see.

Beauty and love,
You'll never miss,
In regards to,
A most passionate kiss.

In the eyes of the beholder,
People are not always blue,
And whoever you meet,
Will always be true.

The imagination is free to soar,
Like the eagle that flies above.
And your heart will never hurt,
From the person you meant to love.

Troubles, no more, lie on your
shoulder.
Only in the eyes of the beholder.

**Altered**

I have changed;
My body feels cold.
I begin to realize,
That I've become too old.

My mind thinks young,
But consider it mistrusted.
If being young is a sin,
Consider me busted.

What I thought was nothing,
Is just where I'm at.
The reason I'm here is something,
That truly killed the cat.

I live for the moment,
But it seems to slip away.
Gentle emotions are here;
Not wanting to stay.

**What's The Matter**

What's the matter now?
Is it me that's so troubled?
Is it hurt from hunger?
Is it our anguish doubled?

What's the matter with us,
That we can't love one another?
Why can't we live peacefully,
With nothing to bother?

What's the matter with them,
Causing us such pain; being
tormented?
Why cause us the trouble?
Their emotions contained; demented.

What's the matter with me?
I seek a love; that is all.
I've hurt so much.
I've hurt myself just to tell you all.

**Inside**

Torn, scathed and bruised,
Nurturing lumpen thought;
I am unaware; used.

Upon the epicene minority,
Burning tear arose on skin,
Falls from slick cheek; guilty.

Soft voice, quiet talk heart,
Stripped of crooked smile,
To emotion impart.

I am not the perfect one,
With rage, I subdue.
To be happy, I hide.
Relinquished thoughts imbued.

# ....Getting rid of some things

**Love is…**

..something untouchable and you cannot see.
..something that is shared between you and me.
..unrealistic in the way we love one another.
..rainy days in which we play; we need nothing but each other.
..intangible feelings that will always be together.
..sharing feelings to communicate better.
..saying I love you when times are hard.
..celebrating tiny things with just a little card.
..trying hard to be sweet and harder to be naughty.
.. a perfect blend of mind and body.

## WOW!!!

Who is that? Who is she? The one I fell for, can't you see? She's true to heart; a tender soul. I like her clearly. I can't let go.
She completes my days; fulfills my thoughts. Just to dream of a kiss. I tend to do that an awful lot.
My beating heart sings to her. Without her smile, my days would blur.
Her beauty shines through her lovely eyes. They stare brilliantly up as through the skies.
I hear her words although by her unspoken. She mends those hearts others left broken.
I imagine her kisses sweet, like Cupid's wine. I'd love to love her until the end of time.
So, who is this that my love has awakened anew? She's the one to which I'd say "I love you."

## Muse

It seemed to be a pattern I traced when I look back upon bittersweet memories of a love that ignited. Just to be a bright reflection inside those eyes…I remember.

Within, a tender song in the tones that bellowed from her whispers. I, loving the warmth of her breath, tingled from the idea of her being close. I remember the sound of my name upon her tongue. And I reflect on the warmth of my heart just to hear her form the word.

I loved the way she carried herself, positive and strong, not letting the convictions of life pull her down. She never tried to be beautiful, she just was. She walked slightly resembling a rhythmic dance that took center stage. Her shadow

displayed on brightest of days was gently poetic to the sun.

Her gentle laugh was caressed from within and hidden behind the simplest of smiles. To be a muse among sinners should have been truly an honor and to her I held most high.

**Made the Mold**

I am a poet, a writer, an artist, a painter, and a comedian.
I am not a church goer but that doesn't mean I am not religious.
I am a lover not a fighter but I have always stood up for love.
I am an impressionist therefore I speak in the name of laughter.
I am simple therefore I need not rich things.
I am complex upon what my heart feels.
I am a father, a son, a brother, and a friend. Therefore, when I am needed, I am there.
I am a romantic therefore I can be deemed hopeless.
I know the pain of being poor but I do not do without.
I have a family of friends that are true to my own heart.
I have a heart that's strong because I've endured through weakness.
I have a love for others for I have been shown how to love.
I am my own person so this makes me priceless.

**Reciprocation**

Sometimes I hate my heart resting there upon my sleeve.
Beating; resounding a rhythm upon the tiniest of drums.
The rhythm…calling me…keeping me from sleep.
Too many times, letting myself fall asleep under the stars I find in other's eyes.
Just letting the hurt escape their hearts and pain float away from their windows.
Putting more stars all over and…seeing something brighter.
I, too, tender from the weight I have chose to bear.
Taking on a little more than I care; away from others.
Letting them know… they are not alone.
My strength, no greater than theirs;
Our hearts, never beating a different song.
It whispers to me; draws my attention.
Take time… you can hear it too.

## Wherever you might be

I realize that it's been a while. It's been a long silence since a text or even one call was answered. An eternity has passed since I have seen you…but lately I have been doing…some thinking.

I try not to think of you as much as I used to. It's not that I regret my past nor do I feel I have to see you again. It's just the weirdest feeling that someone I used to know has utterly become somewhat of a stranger to me.

I choose to forget you most days and then sometimes you're not even a thought for a seemingly long time. It's just easier that way. Maybe… it causes me less pain to have you not so heavy on my heart. I know you wanted the best for me.

The little things haunt me sometimes though. It all comes crashing in around me. I miss you. I think, occasionally, you show up in my dreams. I get vague glimpses now and then.

I thought it would help to write. They say it helps to do such things. I am writing this down in hopes that you have found your way; that you found something that has made you smile. I am writing in hopes that you think of me too. I hope you remember how it was before, before we started to regret.

And yet, it wasn't regret, that's just how things were. It was just how we ended everything as a past familiarity. Maybe, all of this needs to be left unsaid. Maybe you already know these things. Maybe….once upon a time, you started to remember me too.

www.ingramcontent.com/pod-product-compliance
Lightning Source LLC
Chambersburg PA
CBHW071326040426
42444CB00009B/2094